Just an Inch at a Time

(Success, Failure and Achievement)

James Nugent

About the Author

I am an Educator, Author and Adventurer. I have been a teacher for 35 years. I am a certified teacher who is endorsed in: English, Spanish, Psychology, and Special Education. I am also a certified School Counselor. In addition to working for public schools; I worked for 22 years as a part time counselor in private practice. I am a recreational sailor, boater, and citizen scientist. My hobbies are too numerous to list. I am married and have two wonderful grown step-sons.

I invite you to read the following and take any good ideas and apply them to your life. It is the only life you get. Make it excellent and amazing.

Introduction

This is a series of short stories based on true life experiences. Names and identifying characteristics have been changed to avoid embarrassing anybody, except me.

Be that as it may; I am choosing to tell the stories because they contain my secrets to accomplishing an enormous amount of things in my life. I estimate that I have attempted many more things, than I have achieved. Yet, I am quite pleased with the overall outcomes.

This is not a document in which I brag. It is a document in which I share my struggles and accomplishments. You are encouraged to be all which you choose to be. In the end, it only matters what you think about your life and time. Be sure that you don't limit your potential.

My motto

We are what we are

We do what we do

We are nothing less

And nothing more

Than what we choose to be…….

1979 James Nugent

Yes, I am well aware of the grammatical problems in the above statement. But it is my poem and I felt it sounded better this way.

A couple decades later a high school History student of mine got quite angry as he challenged my philosophy. He asked if I really believed the above.

I doubled down and said that for all practical purposes it is true. He again challenged me. What if you want to fly in space? I retorted, "just talk to Burt Rutan in New Mexico." He was building the first private spaceship for the public to fly in space. The student rolled his eyes and became exasperated. It did take several more years to fly his spacecraft in space. The last time I saw the student after graduation; he was a wage slave and had no joy in his life and no particular hope for his future. We are nothing less and nothing more than what we choose to be….

I also agree that, due to things out of our control we cannot achieve some things sometimes. I also know that people often put artificial limits on what they can accomplish.

A lot of the time, people sincerely use dubious excuses to avoid taking responsibility for their lives. People may be lazy, vain or fearful of failing.

It turns out that human limits are vastly higher than we habitually assume. Some people are simply ignorant of their potential. The trick is to enjoy the challenges which one faces when one tries to achieve much more than the average human.

One Caveat

Our human potential is not unlimited; although it may seem unlimited at times. Always remember that a person proposes outcomes yet God determines the outcomes.

Competition

Don't compete with anyone but yourself. We all start at different places in our growth and development, and it is pointless to compete with someone else. It is truly pointless and an illusion to win a competition against someone else. It is better to just be your best. Don't strive for the approval of others. Vanity like this fades quickly. Real excellence is forever and expressed internally. It is who you become that counts in the long term.

Playing Black Jack

I was short on money while I was in graduate school. Having exhausted all my resources I went to a local casino and watched at the beginners table. It was free to watch and warm in the winter. I had no heat in the boat on which I was living. They often gave away free snacks and beverages at the casino. I stayed one night a week for three months. I played thousands of hands of cards in my mind. Then I spent some time with a calculator and developed a method of counting cards.

I noticed that every house rule and player superstition and "bit of player wisdom" would statistically work against the player. I read several Black Jack books and they all advised the exact opposite of my method and most had elaborate mathematical proof that I would lose.

One day I had $60. I sat in "third base" where I could see the table full of cards and began to use my method. I was making minimum bets while a few players were making bets for hundreds of dollars. Other players lost thousands of dollars and I made 50 dollars an hour. They all blamed me for my odd style of playing. They couldn't accept the idea that it was their own fault that they were betting and losing so much money. After ten hours, the casino was closing. I walked away with $505. I went to the casino once a month for two years and only lost my $60 once.

When I married my wife, we paid for the wedding mostly on Black Jack. Then I quit gambling in order to be a good role model for family and friends. Nowadays I intermittently play just for fun and to see if my method still works☺ It does.

I learned a lot about life and success from Black Jack.

-Knowing the rules is important.

I studied the rules and figured how they help the house. There are some Black Jack games I won't play. Like life some games, can be rigged against you. Never play a rigged game.

-Do Your Homework.

I flunked statistics 3 times in my life. However, that did not stop me from eventually figuring the odds of the next card the dealer had.

-Listen to the "wisdom and superstition "of other people. Then get them out of your head.

-Ignore naysayers. If I ever gave into negative people I would never accomplish anything!

-Set your loss limits and walk away when it is time. In this way you will always win in a way.

-Be willing to sit there for however long it takes; even if people are angry and you are have to breath smoke.

-Enjoy the drama and the fun of it all.

The rest of this booklet will examine these lessons learned from life and Black Jack. The stories are true and kind of fun.

Know the rules

I have attended courses and or degree programs in excess of 12 different colleges and universities. I always read the school catalogue cover to cover. It gives me a wealth of ideas and information. This information is the rule book by which you and the school must live.

For instance, in undergraduate school I noticed that there was no limit to how many credits I could take. Any credits over 18 were free. So, I would intermittently take a few extra credits and I was able to graduate with a double major in Criminal Justice and English Literature and a teaching certificate. This was even more impressive because I needed to use the last semester exclusively for my student teaching experience.

Over the following years, I found other "loopholes" in other schools that rewarded me many free and super cheap credits. I have studied catalogues all my adult life, to my gain. Classes are expensive.

They cost round $1000 dollars or more. I don't know how many credits I have these days, but I guess perhaps I have 300 college credits. Most of them were cheap or free.

I recently discovered a loophole in the local college catalogue. If you are 60 years or older you can take up to 8 credits at a time for free. I have always wanted to learn to draw. So two years from now I will take an introduction to drawing. I have no idea if I can do it or not. If I succeed I will then put my heart into the project. I will become an artist.

If I gain the skill; I will draw portraits in the local farmer's market and enter art shows. I would love to sell one drawing and have it publically displayed somewhere. It will be an adventure, indeed!

What if it doesn't work out?

It is all in fun.

Exactly what do I have to lose?

Nothing!

What do I have to gain?

Hopefully I will learn to draw basic illustrations for my books. Also I have recently wanted to draw and publish graphic novels (comic books) on Amazon.

Knowing the rules is super important in life.

Knowing the facts

So how did a guy who flunked statistics three time figure out the probabilities involved in Black Jack. It was fairly easy. I asked myself the questions I wanted to know and then read the small section on probability in and old textbook. Nowadays, I would use the internet to carefully find the facts. If I couldn't figure it out on my own I would have asked a college professor how to do it.

Undersea Adventure

I am a diver and live near Puget Sound. I got it in my mind to that I wanted to build an undersea station in Puget Sound. I studied via the internet, the history and the physiology of undersea living. Then I design a simple habitat that would do the job.

When I bought pieces of equipment for my project; I made sure that everything which I bought had a dual purpose. For example, I bought a cheap generator that would also power my home in a power outage.

As part of my research; I spoke with experts around the country. I even went to Florida and spent the night in an underwater habitat and got to drive a remote controlled underwater vehicle. I also toured a tiny operating underwater research station. I became an officially certified PADI aquanaut. An aquanaut is a person who spends 24 hours underwater.

The only thing I regret about the experiences is that I watched a DVD called "The Abyss" while staying alone on the seafloor at night. It is a scary movie when you are underwater!

I wrote a short book about the trip to Florida. The book is called, "Twenty Hours under the Sea". I was really going to put an underwater facility in Puget Sound and connect it to classrooms via the internet. It would have been emplaced right off the beach at my house on Young Cove. I was really flying so high.

Then, medical problems struck and I was out of the water and disabled for a long time. I never again could get anybody else excited about the project. It is shelved for now. I still have things like the generator in my garage ready for when the lights go out!

Failure

Although it was never deployed; I do not consider my undersea project a failure. It just was not ever completed. I had great adventures and was only $4000 away from having a rudimentary working undersea station. I was about to buy quick cement for ballast to anchor the system to the sea floor. I suddenly developed potentially lethal medical issues.

Everything I try accomplish is done just a little at a time. I have been called relentless when I go after a goal. I guess nothing is really over until I quite or I die.

An inch at a time

When I was a teen; an old man told me I could have an old wooden boat if I would just take it off his property on Puget Sound. I found that I could slide the beast on planks on the ground. I put Crisco Oil on the planks and could push it about 1 inch at a time. It was 22 feet long and about 1200 pounds. I moved it 2 feet a day for about 6 weeks. Then I carefully patched a big hole in the boat and paddled the boat away.

What I learned was patience. It is the same patience I used when a played Black Jack for living. The same restful attentiveness was needed when working with counseling clients in private part time practice for twenty-two years. It is the same diligence needed to learn from numerous diverse professors in order to become a school counselor or Spanish teacher or Special Education teacher over the last 35 years. Being able to happily work and wait for years to achieve a goal is a critical skill.

After my medical issues struck, I doubted if I could teach again. It turned out that I was wrong. However, at the time I immediately started a new career, as a writer self-publishing at Amazon. Some of my books were mediocre when I started, but I have greatly improved. Five years later I now have published 118 e-books, 110 paperbacks and 56 audio books. When I get to 500 hundred products I will retire, or perhaps I will go on to write 1000 books. Most of my books are around 28 pages long. The minimum length for a paperback is 24 pages. I do enjoy writing so much.

Dealing with Negative People

Other people can convince you fail before you even get started! One of my many joys in life has been song writing. I have written and performed more than 50 musical works of art. I even have a couple songs for sale on a CD at Amazon. They are performed by a professional performer, Erin McNamee. This was one of my lifelong dreams.

I wanted to be a published songwriter but it almost never happened when I was 18 years-old. A friend, thoughtlessly laughed at me, and insulted my songs. It was devastating. I didn't pick up a guitar for 6 months. Eventually I got my muse back and shared my songs with many thousands of children and in turn they sang my songs to their children. My music goes on like ripples in a huge sea of life. Sometimes, nowadays, when I don't feel particularly successful; I just go to the nearest device, get a free download of my music and then I remember. I remember that I have achieved so many of my dreams.

Always follow your bliss. Reject anybody's opinion who tries to stop you.

Another Example

Five years ago when I was convalescing and barely able to sit up a few hours a day; I was writing. A well-meaning relative got hysterical. She said, I would never make a living, writing books. I instantly told her that it was all I could do for now. I was writing for my own pleasure and therapy. It was not unlike when I used to sing. I am so grateful that I knew not to let somebody sabotage my writing.

Why do people try to sabotage others?

-Some people accidentally put barriers in your way.

-Some people are jealous.

-Some people are just afraid.

-Some people are wicked.

-Some people are afraid that if you succeed; they will have no excuse for not doing something of their own.

Be sure to forgive all who try to frustrate your goals. You don't want to carry any burdens as you move on. Be sure to thank all people who are supportive. What goes around seems to come around.

People are Resources

If you want to know anything nowadays; you can reach almost everybody e-mail. In many adventures as a citizen scientist I have been able to query the actual by scientists who are doing cutting edge science.

Experts will almost always respond to your questions and direct you to other resources. An example of the many people I have e-mailed is Chris (his real name). He is the holder of the record for the most days spent underwater over several decades.

He is typical of the wonderful people who have helped me in my adventuring. Chris and I exchanged many e-mails and he was instrumental in giving me key bits of information which were critical in the design of my underwater station for Puget Sound.

In contrast to the undersea station project; I did not get a response from a group which does Mars Analog missions. I was Interested in being a member of mission control. I would work from home while they do mock up missions in a far flung desert. In a way this just forces me to get more creative in how I might contact these good people. My secret dream is to actually go on a mission simulation, wear spacesuits and perform work as a communication specialist. I am a licensed amateur radio operator. Of course, I would publish a diary of the mission experience and do a Ham Radio magazine article. It is all for fun.

Recommendation

Don't disclose to most people what you are trying to achieve. They just won't understand or will even mock you.

Summary

Let your mind wonder outside the box in which we normally live. I like to just play a game on the internet. I start with a single search term on any topic. I spend hours reading about the topic. When I feel like I have exhausted my interest in that topic; I search a related term or topic. Eventually I stumble upon something I don't know about. Then I figure out how I might participate.

Sometimes this might involve going to school online in order to get a certification or some training in a topic. With my new certifications I am often qualified to participate in all sort of interesting stuff. I almost never pay for this education.

For example, FEMA has hundreds of online classes for free. If you need actual college credit you can even get real college credit for $49 at a cooperating school. If you just need the classes, you can do it for free and be issued a FEMA Certificates.

Hundreds of public and private agencies have what I call shadow education systems. Shadow education systems of highly focused collections of classes which the agency or employer needs the employees to master. Many are absolutely free or very cheap to the public.

For example, years ago I was contacted by a private company that had dozens of free classes for employees. The classes were accessed through their public website. They wanted to know why I was taking their free Chinese language classes. I was not an employee. I ended up directing an English/Chinese Summer Institute for three years. I never did learn to speak Chinese very well.

The online opportunities are nearly endless. One interesting website with excellent classes for free of cheap is Coursera. The classes are offered by Universities from all over the world.

Also, I often audit classes and workshops for free at Universities or Colleges. I am seriously interested in visiting some of the great telescopes of the world. I plan to audit astronomy classes and then become an intern and go to various institutions with world-class telescopes. If I need to actually take a class for credit; it will be an upper division class and I will pay for it with money from a website that has a billion dollars in scholarships for students. Fastweb.com is how I paid for my Special Education Teaching Endorsement.

At any particular time; I am working two or three plans to achieve one or two personal goals.

Final Comments

Once you try something outside your comfort zone, you will enjoy the process. You will not always succeed. For example I failed (statistics) in one grad school before I found a school that didn't have the math requirement. By the way, nowadays there is a simple computer application for statistics in sciences which does your statistics for you.

Anyway, in the first school I spent the winter living in the Psychology building (it was winter) and working as a TA for a Professor who recognized that I had successfully taught myself applied Rational Psychology. His recommendations were a golden ticket to many other adventures.

I got to talk with world famous thinkers in the field of Counseling Psychology. All I needed to be privy to meeting these people was a suit and tie from the thrift store. Also, I needed a letter of introduction from my department and a pair of used loafers from my friend. I was at that University for 6 months. It was the most fun I ever had failing at school. Then again it wasn't really failing.

Formal brick and mortar schools are not really my strong suit. I learn best in hands on situations. I went for free to an institute on Satellite Communications for two summers. I learned to build devices and robots. I learned to use satellite communications and learned to make robots do what I wanted them to do. I went to Language Emersion Programs for a total of 5 months and learned Esperanto while receiving 6 college credits. I taught myself to SCUBA dive/ Commercial dive and worked as a paid diver for a summer. I was a paid Red Cross First Aid/ CPR Instructor for a while. I taught myself Spanish by traveling in Latin American and took correspondence Spanish classes. Eventually, I was qualified as a Spanish Teacher. I learned to fly a small plan. I taught myself to sail and kayak. I taught myself to rock climb. I could list 100 more things I have learned in non-traditional ways. There are many more things to learn on my bucket list.

The point is to find something that looks interesting and do it. Enjoy the process of making your way to a new outcome. Gain new skills and knowledge. Go for the joy of it.

A Last Thought

I saw a real inch worm on my back deck today. I fell asleep in the shade and I dreamed about his lonely life of struggle. An hour later I awoke. He was way up a small tree resting in the cool breeze. I thought, life is not so bad, one inch at a time.

Books by James Nugent

Just an Inch at a Time

A Canoe trip from Hammersley Inlet to Hope Island

A Guide for the Beginning School Teacher

A Guide to Effective Communication in Catholic Parishes

Eucharistic Adoration

Puget Sound Mud Mucking

Garage Sales for Fun and Profit

Super Summer Camp Counseling

Fourteen Years as a Eucharistic Visitor

With the Tides and Wind (lessons Learned from Sailing for Life)

Against the Tide (A Story about Love and a Boat)

Trusting God

Homelessness Survival Stories

Substitute Teaching in Juvenile Detention

Why Take the Risk?

The House on Gallagher way

A Beginners Adventures in Archery

The Surviving Spouse

Writing Interesting E-books

A Catholic's View of Sin

My Boat My Vacation

Fifty-Two Vacations a Year

Writing Interesting E-books

My Boat My Vacation

An Idea Called Camp Gallagher

Finding Meaning in Retirement

Adventures on the Olympia Harbor Patrol

Catholic Way of Suffering

E-book Writing and My Search for Inspiration

The Joy of Cats

Thank You

Living on the Edge of Civilization

How I Sailed from Olympia to the San Juan Islands, and Returned Safely

An Alternative Boating Guide to Southern Puget Sound

Twenty Hours under the Sea

Without Speech

Miracles in Young Cove

Home Self-defense

How and Why I Lived Aboard

Kayaking Budd Inlet in South Puget Sound

Writing E-books and Making the Perfect Book

I Speak Esperanto

The Rainbow Road and Other Signs of God's Love

Write a Book

Living an Abundant Life, Within Your Means

Crazy Making

Social Jujitsu and Powerful Principles for Managing Social Conflict

Advanced Social Jujitsu

Blackjack on My Small Budget

A Little Benedictine Oblate Manuel

Without Speech

All things work

Loving Time with Your Creator

Personal Adventures in a Life of Learning

Loving Time with Your Creator

The Good News about Being Catholic

The Extraordinary Eucharistic Visitor

E-book Writing and Overcoming Barriers to Creativity

Living an Abundant Life; Within Your Means

E-book Writing and Organizing Your Ideas

Paddling to the Rhythm of God

My Forty Days for Life 2013 Lifestyle Reality Observing

How to Sail in the Winter

How to Get Your Kid to Move Out

How to Get What Want

Sex, Abstinence, and Happiness

Cynthia Says Radio Show – Anger is a choice

Eight Things You Need to Survive

Three Moms from Hell

Moving and Starting Fresh

More Good News about Being Catholic

The Solo Kayak

Everyday Survival Kit

Rainy Day Kayak

Night Kayak

Solo Kayak II

Paddles and Water

A Beach Naturalist on Southern Puget Sound

Clean House Clean Life

The Total Catholic Christian

Advanced Social Jujitsu

The Beginning School Counselor

Managing the Most Difficult Students

Taking Responsibility

The Friends You Keep

Happiness is a Choice

Why Write?

The Voyages of Saint Bernadett

Available at Amazon.com in: E-Book and or Audible Book or Paperback. All rights reserved. Copyrights 2018. Eld Inlet Services.

28

www.ingramcontent.com/pod-product-compliance
Lightning Source LLC
Chambersburg PA
CBHW051411250726
48656CB00010B/2328